Janice VanCleave's
EARTHQUAKES

JANICE VANCLEAVE'S
SPECTACULAR SCIENCE PROJECTS

Animals
Earthquakes
Gravity
Machines
Magnets
Molecules

JANICE VANCLEAVE'S
SCIENCE FOR EVERY KID SERIES

Astronomy for Every Kid
Biology for Every Kid
Chemistry for Every Kid
Earth Science for Every Kid
Math for Every Kid
Physics for Every Kid

...ular Science Projects

Janice VanCleave's
EARTHQUAKES

Mind-boggling Experiments You Can Turn Into Science Fair Projects

John Wiley & Sons, Inc.
New York • Chichester • Brisbane • Toronto • Singapore

Design and Production by Navta Associates, Inc.
Illustrated by Ray Burns

Library of Congress Cataloging-in-Publication Data
VanCleave, Janice Pratt.
  [Earthquakes]
  Janice VanCleave's earthquakes.
  p. cm. — (Spectacular Science Projects)
  Includes index.
  Summary: A collection of science projects and experiments exploring various aspects of earthquakes.
  ISBN 0-471-57107-5 (pbk.)
  1. Earthquakes—Juvenile literature. [1. Earthquakes—Experiments. 2. Experiments. 3. Science projects.] I. Title. II. Title: Earthquakes. III. Series: VanCleave, Janice Pratt. Janice VanCleave's spectacular science projects.
QE521.3.V37   1993
551.2 '2'078—dc20   92-29089

Printed in the United States of America
10 9 8 7

CONTENTS

God has brought three special people into
our family, and it is an honor for me to dedicate this
book to them,
Ginger and Tina VanCleave, and Calvin Russell

Introduction

Science is a search for answers. Science projects are good ways to learn more about science as you search for the answers to specific problems. This book will give you guidance and provide ideas, but you must do your part in the search by planning experiments, finding and recording information related to the problem, and organizing the data collected to find the answer to the problem. Sharing your findings by presenting your project at science fairs will be a rewarding experience if you have properly prepared for the exhibit. Trying to assemble a project overnight results in frustration, and you cheat yourself out of the fun of being a science detective. Solving a scientific mystery, like solving a detective mystery, requires planning and the careful collecting of facts. The following sections provide suggestions for how to get started on this scientific quest. Start the project with curiosity and a desire to learn something new.

SELECT A TOPIC

The 20 topics in this book suggest many possible problems to solve. Each topic has one "cookbook" experiment—follow the recipe and the result is guaranteed. Approximate metric equivalents have been given after all English measurements. Try several or all of these easy experiments before choosing the topic you like best and want to know more about. Regardless of the problem you choose to solve, what you discover will make you more knowledgeable about earthquakes.

KEEP A JOURNAL

Purchase a bound notebook in which you will write everything relating to the project. This is your journal. It will contain your original ideas as well as ideas you get from books or from people like teachers and scientists. It will include descriptions of your experiments as well as diagrams, photographs, and written observations of all your results. Every entry should be as neat as possible and dated. Information from this journal can be used to write a report of your project, and you will want to display the journal with your completed project. A neat, orderly journal provides a complete and accurate record of your project from start to finish. It is also proof of the time you spent sleuthing out the answers to the scientific mystery you undertook to solve.

LET'S EXPLORE

This section of each chapter follows each of the 20 sample experiments and provides additional questions about the problem presented in the experiment. By making small changes to some part of the sample experiment, new results are achieved. Think about why these new results might have happened.

SHOW TIME!

You can use the pattern of the sample experiment to design your own experiments to solve the questions asked in "Let's Explore." Your own experiment should follow the sample experiment's format and include a single question about one idea, a list of necessary materials, a detailed step-by-step procedure, written results with diagrams, graphs, and charts if they seem helpful, and a conclusion answering and explaining the question. Include any information you found through research to clarify your answer. When you design your own experiments, make sure to get adult approval if supplies or procedures other than those given in this book are used.

If you want to make a science fair project, study the information listed here and after each sample experiment in the book to develop your ideas into a real science fair exhibit. Use the suggestions that best apply to the project topic that you have chosen. Keep in mind that while your display represents all the work that you have done, it must tell the story of the project in such a way that it attracts and holds the interest of the viewer. So keep it simple. Do not try to cram all of your information into one place. To have more space on the display and still exhibit all your work, keep some of the charts, graphs, pictures, and other materials in

your journal instead of on the display board itself.

The actual size and shape of displays can be different, depending on the local science fair officials, so you will have to check the rules for your science fair. Most exhibits are allowed to be 48 inches (122 cm) wide, 30 inches (76 cm) deep, and 108 inches (274 cm) high. These are maximum measurements and your display may be smaller than this. A three-sided backboard (see drawing) is usually the best way to display your work. Wooden panels can be hinged together, but you can also use sturdy cardboard pieces taped together to form a very inexpensive but presentable exhibit.

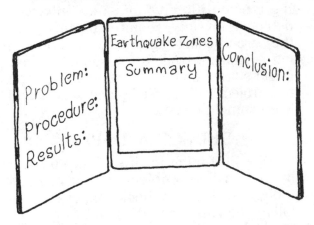

A good title of six words or less with a maximum of 50 characters should be placed at the top of the center panel. The title should capture the theme of the project but should not be the same as the problem statement. For example, if the problem under question is *Where are earthquakes most likely to occur?,* a good title for the project may be "Earthquake Zones." The title and other headings should be neat and large enough to be readable at a distance of about 3 feet (1 meter). You can glue letters to the backboard (you can use precut letters that you buy or letters that you cut out of construction paper), or you can stencil the letters for all the titles. A short summary paragraph of about 100 words to explain the scientific principles involved is good and can be printed under the title. A person who has no knowledge of the topic should be able to easily understand the basic idea of the project just from reading the summary.

There are no set rules about the position of the information on the display. However, it all needs to be well organized, with the title and summary paragraph as the main point at the top of the center panel and the remaining material placed neatly from left to right under specific headings. Choices of headings will depend on how you wish to display the information. Separate headings for Problem, Procedure, Results, and Conclusion may be used.

The judges give points for how clearly you are able to discuss the project and explain its purpose, procedure, results, and conclusion. The display should be organized so that it explains everything, but your ability to discuss your project and answer the questions of the judges convinces them that you did the work and understand what you have done. Practice a speech in front of friends, and invite them to ask you questions. If you do not know the answer to a question, never guess or make up an answer or just say, "I do not know." Instead, you can say that you did not discover that answer during your research and then offer other information that you found of interest about the project. Be proud of the project and approach the judges with enthusiasm about your work.

CHECK IT OUT!

Read about your topic in many books and magazines. You are more likely to have a successful project if you are well informed about the topic. For the topics in this book, some tips are provided about specific places to look for information. Record in your journal all the information you find, and include for each source the author's name, the book title (or magazine name and article title), the numbers of the pages you read, the publisher's name, where it was published, and the year of publication.

Old Myths

PROBLEM

According to Aristotle, how were earth-quakes produced?

Materials

long balloon
2 books

Procedure

1. Lay a long balloon on a table with the mouth of the balloon hanging over the table's edge.

2. Place the two books end to end on top of the balloon.

3. Inflate the balloon by blowing into it.

4. Release the opening and allow the air to escape quickly.

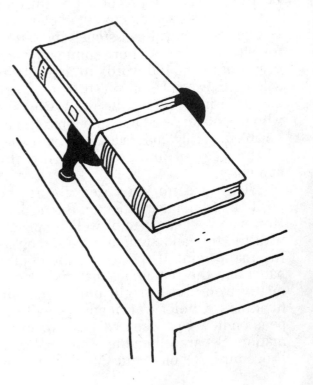

Results

Inflating the balloon causes the books to rise and separate. The books fall—but not necessarily into their original position—when the balloon deflates.

Why?

Your exhaled breath—a gas—moves into and fills the balloon. The gas pushes the rubbery walls of the balloon in all directions, and thus forces them outward. As the balloon expands, the books rise and separate. Removal of the gas from the balloon allows the books to return to their normal level, but to a different position. More than 2,000 years ago a Greek philosopher, Aristotle, proposed that gases trapped in caves beneath the earth's surface expanded when heated. He believed that the expanded gas pushed on the inside walls of the caves, forcing them to move, thereby causing earthquakes. Scientists have since discovered that this is not the case, as you will see in later experiments.

LET'S EXPLORE

1. Could the size of the underground caverns have been thought to affect the **magnitude** (shaking energy) of the earthquakes? Repeat the experiment twice, first using a larger balloon, and then using a smaller balloon. **Science Fair Hint:** Display diagrams and/or photographs of each experiment.

2. How would different land masses be affected by the expanding caverns? Repeat the original experiment, replacing the books with a layer of dirt. Repeat a second time using a layer of clay across the balloon. **Science Fair Hint:** Use each type of land mass tested and the results as part of a project display.

3. Anaxagoras, another ancient Greek philosopher, reasoned that earthquake motion was caused when the sections of the earth cracked and fell into the earth's empty core. This can be demonstrated by repeating the original experiment, tying the inflated balloon, and then using a stickpin to break it. How do the books move when the balloon is broken?

SHOW TIME!

Until the 20th century, the causes of earthquakes remained a profound mystery. Find out more about past and present beliefs about the causes of earthquakes. Display pictures and diagrams of these modern and ancient ideas. One example is that throughout the centuries many people thought that the earth rested on the back of an animal such as a turtle, whose occasional motion caused the world to tremble. Display a diagram representing a turtle with the earth on its back. A model could be constructed using a toy animal and a large ball painted to represent the earth.

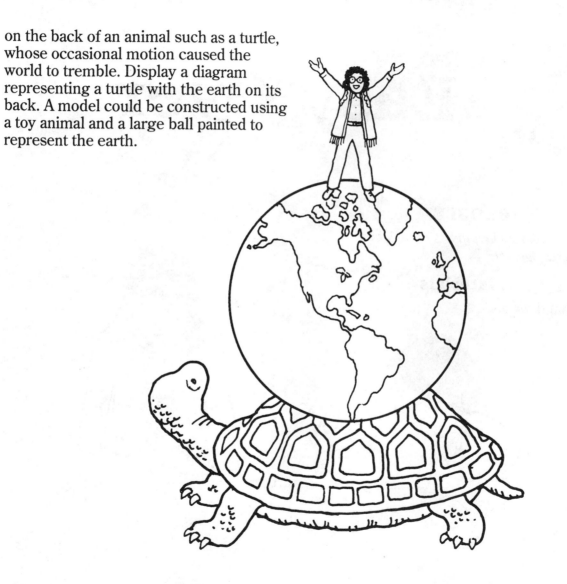

Easy Over

PROBLEM

What happens when layers of rock are squeezed together?

Materials

4 hand towels

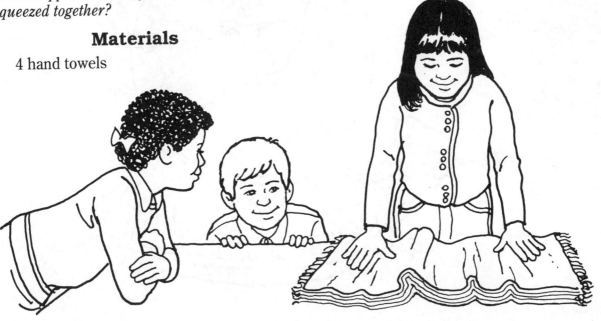

Procedure

1. Stack the outstretched towels on a table.

2. Place your hands on opposite ends of the towels.

3. Slowly push the ends of the towels about 4 inches (10 cm) toward the center.

4. Observe the shape of the towels.

Results

The towels form folds.

Why?

Pushing from opposite directions causes the towels to be squeezed into shapes called folds. The result is a surface with a wavelike appearance. Forces pushing toward each other from opposite directions are called **compression forces**. Such forces within the earth can crush rocks like a mighty nutcracker, and can slowly squeeze rock layers into folds like those of the stack of towels. If the compression force is applied quickly, the rocks break, producing earthquakes.

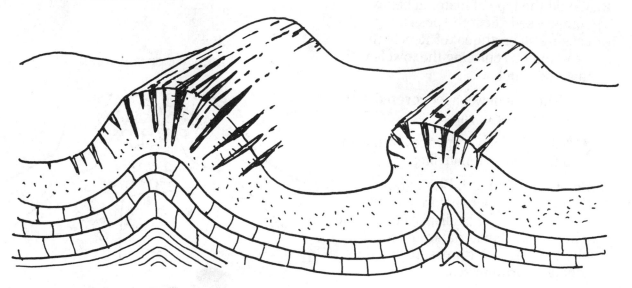

LET'S EXPLORE

1. Does the amount of force affect the results? Repeat the experiment twice, first pushing your hands *less* than 4 inches (10 cm) toward the center, and then pushing them *more* than 4 inches (10 cm) toward the center. **Science Fair Hint:** Photographs and/or diagrams showing the difference in the results can be used as part of a project display.

2. Would the type of material being compressed affect the possibility of causing an earthquake? Repeat the experiment, replacing the towels with materials such as:

   - a sheet of newspaper covered with a thin layer of sand.
   - a sheet of newspaper covered with a thin layer of modeling clay.

   Science Fair Hint: Photographs of the covered papers before and after compression can be displayed. Indicate which type of material would most likely break under pressure and thus produce earthquakes.

SHOW TIME!

1. Demonstrate how compression force crushes different materials. Cover a table with a sheet of newspaper. Place a testing material between the palms of your hands. Hold your hands over the newspaper so that any falling particles land on it. Push your hands together as hard and as fast as possible, making an effort to crush the material. Observe each material tested and describe the results. Test these items:

   - a slice of bread.
   - a cracker.
   - a cookie.
   - an empty ice cream cone.

2. Demonstrate how compression forces create folds by pushing on both ends of a large sponge. Use this as part of an oral demonstration. Diagrams of the results can be displayed.

CHECK IT OUT!

A mountain is a rock mass rising more than 2,000 feet (610 m) above the surrounding land. The Appalachians, the Rockies, the Himalayas, and the Alps are all examples of folded mountain ranges that were formed by compression forces. Read about folded mountain ranges, including any evidence of earthquakes in these regions.

3

Jolted

PROBLEM

How do faults produce earthquakes?

Materials

2 wooden blocks, each about 2 inches
   × 4 inches × 6 inches (5 cm × 10 cm
   × 15 cm)
2 sheets of medium-grade sandpaper
masking tape

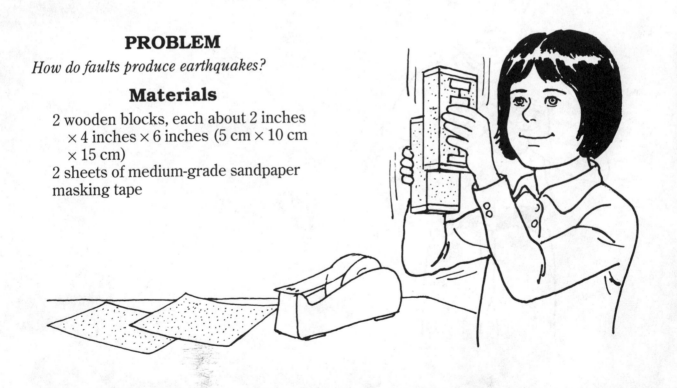

Procedure

1. Wrap each wooden block with a sheet of sandpaper, and secure with tape.

2. Hold one block in each hand. The blocks should be held straight up and down.

3. Push the blocks together tightly.

4. While continuing to push the blocks together, try to slide the blocks in different directions.

Results

The sandpaper-covered blocks temporarily lock together and then move with a jolt.

Why?

The **lithosphere** (the solid, outermost part of the earth's surface) is broken into major sections referred to as **tectonic plates**. Where the edges of two plates push against each other, the crack between the plates is called a **fault**. **Friction** (the resistance to motion) causes the plates to be temporarily locked together. Faults that are temporarily locked together are called **lock faults**. The two blocks of wood represent two tectonic plates pushing against each other. They temporarily lock together, but as with actual tectonic plates, the friction between the blocks eventually fails, causing a sudden jolt. The bond holding a locked fault in place is under tremendous stress, but may last for years before suddenly slipping. Lock faults inevitably and frequently fail, resulting in an explosion of motion that produces powerful earthquakes.

LET'S EXPLORE

1. Would the size of the rocks in a fault area affect slippage? Repeat the experiment twice, first covering the blocks with a fine grade of sandpaper, and again using a coarse grade of sandpaper. **Science Fair Hint:** Use different wooden blocks for each experiment, and include the blocks as part of a project display.

2. Does the size of the areas pushing against each other affect the bond between the blocks? Repeat the original experiment twice more, first using smaller blocks, and then using larger blocks. **Science Fair Hint:** Display the blocks used along with the results.

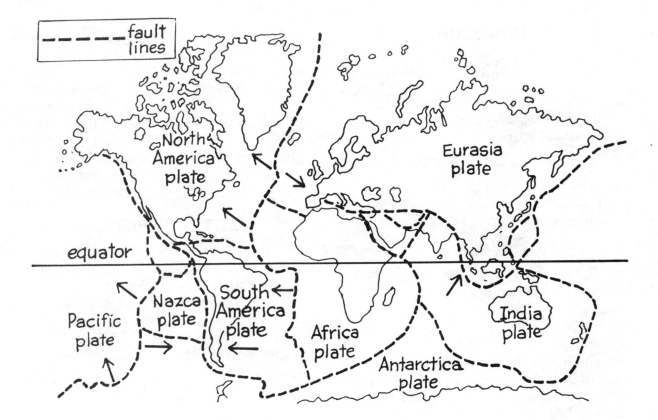

SHOW TIME!

1. How might a **lubricant** (slippery material) affect the bond between a lock fault? With your hand, push the bottom of a tennis shoe against a tile floor. Try to slide the shoe forward while continuing to push the shoe against the floor. With a parent's permission, repeat the experiment, placing several tablespoons of water on the tile under the shoe. Display photographs of this experiment along with the results.

Write a **hypothesis** (an educated guess) as to how you think lubricants, such as water or mud, would affect the bond between lock faults. *NOTE: Be sure to use a paper towel to remove the water from the tile.*

2. You can create a more detailed model of a lock fault, and display it with an explanation of its parts. Stack layers of different colors of modeling clay. Cut the clay layers diagonally. Insert marbles into the clay pieces so that the marbles touch, making it difficult for the two clay halves to slip past each other.

CHECK IT OUT!

Faults slip and produce earthquakes. Some faults are constantly moving at a very slow rate and are called *creeping faults*. The Wayward fault in California is an example of a creeping fault. Is a creeping fault less likely to slip and result in an earthquake? Find out more about faults, their movements, and their locations.

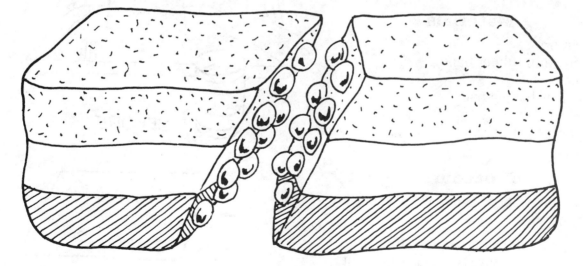

4

Snap!

PROBLEM

How does the rebounding of stretched rocks cause earthquakes?

Materials

scissors
long, thin rubber band
ruler
shallow baking pan
helper
sheet of paper
salt

Procedure

1. Cut the rubber band to make a long strip.

2. Measure the length of the strip with the ruler. Be sure that the strip is not stretched while measuring.

BEFORE

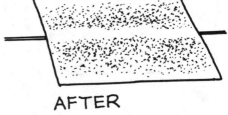

AFTER

3. Hold the ends of the rubber strip against the bottom of the baking pan.

4. Ask a helper to lay a sheet of paper over the rubber strip and to cover the area of the paper directly above the strip with a thin layer of salt.

5. Hold the rubber strip tightly and pull your hands apart as far as possible without breaking the strip.

6. Release both ends of the rubber strip at the same time.

7. Observe and record the results.

8. Measure the length of the rubber strip again without stretching it.

Results

The particles of salt move slightly as the rubber strip is stretched, but are thrown in different directions when the strip is released. A trough is formed in the salt layer directly above the rubber band. The rubber strip is longer after being stretched.

Why?

Your hands and the rubber strip form one continuous unit before the strip breaks away from your fingers. The movement of the rubber strip as it stretches taps against the paper, causing the salt particle to separate. As the molecules in the rubber strip are pulled apart, the **potential energy** (energy due to position) inside the strip increases. This potential energy is quickly changed to **kinetic energy** (energy of motion) when the ends of the strip pull away from your fingers and the rubber strip snaps back to an unstrained position. This sudden release of energy causes the strip to **vibrate** (move back and forth).

Like the rubber strip, when a section of the earth's surface is pulled or pushed upon, it stretches, causing great pressure inside the rocks. When the strain becomes too great, the rocks suddenly break and snap back to an unstrained position. The sudden movements and the scraping of the rocks past each other as they **rebound** (snap back) make the earth shake violently. This motion is called an **earthquake**. After the vibrations cease, some of the stretched but unbroken rocks return to their original shape.

Like the rubber strip, some rocks that have been stretched too far are permanently deformed.

LET'S EXPLORE

1. Does the amount of strain affect the change in the length of the material being stretched? Repeat the experiment using rubber bands of the same size. Change the distance that each rubber strip is stretched before releasing. **Science Fair Hint:** As part of a display, attach the rubber strips used in the experiments to a sheet of paper. Record any change in length next to each rubber strip.

2. Is the amount of vibration affected by the type of rebounding material? Repeat the experiment using different types of material, such as string, thread, and pieces of sewing elastic. The materials used, along with the results, can be part of a project display.

SHOW TIME!

1. Grasp the ends of a plastic ruler in each hand. Push down on the ends, bending the ruler in an arc. Stop pushing down on the ruler, and

describe the rebounding movement of the ruler within your hands. A photograph showing the arc in the ruler can be part of a project display. Add a description of the results and how this type of movement in the earth's crust creates earthquakes.

balloon stretch more than others, causing a change in the shape of the square drawn on the balloon. Deflate the balloon and measure the square. Experiment with different amounts of inflation to determine how big the balloon has to stretch before it will not rebound to its original size.

2. Demonstrate that solids in the earth's crust that have elastic properties can recover their original shape and size when forces are not too strong. Use a marking pen to draw a 2-inch × 2-inch (4-cm × 4-cm) square on a deflated, round balloon. Inflate the balloon slightly and observe the position of the marks. Make a diagram of the inflated balloon to show that some parts of the

CHECK IT OUT!

Find out more about the *Elastic Rebound Theory*. Who developed it, and when? You could use this theory in the conclusion of a report about your project explaining how rocks in the earth's surface move, causing earthquakes.

5

Recycle

PROBLEM

Where are earthquakes most likely to occur?

Materials

scissors
sheet of typing paper
ruler
shoe box
marking pen

Procedure

1. Cut a piece of typing paper into three equally long strips.

2. Measure and cut out two ½-inch × 4-inch (1-cm × 10-cm) sections in the bottom of the box about 4 inches (10 cm) apart.

3. Use the marking pen to label the slits as A and B.

4. On one of the box's largest sides, cut out a section large enough to insert your hands.

5. Put two of the paper strips together, and pull them up through slit A in the box.

6. Pull the strips out (be sure to leave a few inches inside the box). Bend them apart and insert one strip down through slit B as in the diagram.

7. Push the end of the third paper strip down through slit B.

8. Hold the strips under the box between your index and second fingers of each hand.

9. Slowly pull down on the paper strips in slit A while pushing the strips in slit B upward.

Results

The paper pieces move toward each other as they slip down through slit A. At slit B, the paper pieces rise out of the slit and move away from each other in opposite directions.

Why?

The earth's **lithosphere** (the solid, outermost part of the earth) is believed to be broken into several major sections or plates—North America, South America, Eurasia, Africa, India, Antarctica, Nazca, and Pacific. Each major plate is broken into smaller sections. The shoe-box model demonstrates the movement of the plates at the ocean ridges. The rising paper acts like hot molten rock moving out of the cracks in the midocean ridge. When **magma** (liquid rock) pushes through the ocean floor's surface, it forms a new layer on both sides of the crack. This new material spreads the ocean floors apart.

As the ocean widens, the bordering continents move apart, but the earth does not change in size. The earth is constantly recycling itself as new material forms and older parts of its lithosphere sink. Ocean trenches form where sections of the lithosphere are pushed together, forcing one of the plates downward and below the opposing plate. These areas of sinking lithosphere are called **subduction zones**. Earthquakes are more common anywhere the lithosphere plates move, but the subduction zones have the largest number of earthquakes and volcanic activity. The reason for this intense activity at subduction zones is that great pressures are produced as the plates rub against each other.

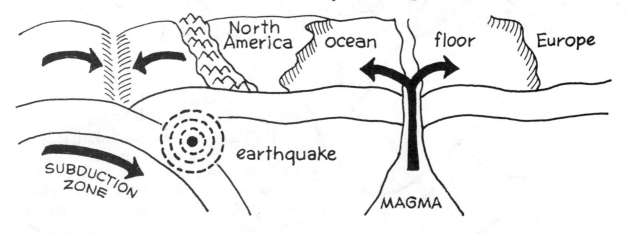

LET'S EXPLORE

1. What happens if the old lithosphere is not removed at the same rate that new lithosphere is added? Repeat the experiment, pushing the paper up faster at slit B than you pull the papers down at slit A.

2. How would a fracture in one of the plates affect the results? Repeat the original experiment after cutting the entire length of the paper strip between slits A and B lengthwise. Be sure that only two strips are being moved through each slit.

SHOW TIME!

1. Plate spreading, plate subduction, and plate sliding are different types of plate movements. A way to display the differences in these movements would be with a diagram showing all three examples. Use arrows to indicate the direction of plate movement in each example.

2. Display shoebox models to represent the three types of plate boundaries: those at fractures, where plates slide past each other; those at the ocean ridges, where plates are pulled apart and new material rises; and those at ocean trenches, where the plates are pushed together and sink.

CHECK IT OUT!

LAGEOS (Laser Geodynamic Satellite) is a satellite that orbits the earth. Find out more about how this satellite, along with a laser device on the ground, is used to track and measure the movement of the earth's crust.

More than 90 percent of all energy released by earthquakes occurs in the Pacific Ring of Fire. Find out more about the location of this area.

6

Quake Center

PROBLEM

Where on the earth's surface is the strongest shaking of an earthquake felt?

Materials

adult helper
saw
wooden block measuring about 2
    inches × 4 inches × 8 inches (5 cm ×
    10 cm × 20 cm)
metal cookie sheet
¼ cup (60 ml) garden soil
large metal spoon

Procedure

1. Ask an adult to saw the wooden block in half diagonally.

2. Hold the two pieces of the block together and set them on a metal cookie sheet.

3. Position the cookie sheet so that the beginning of the break between the wooden pieces is over the edge of a table.

4. Cover the tops of the wooden pieces with a layer of soil.

5. Use the metal spoon to tap on the cookie sheet just below the break between the wooden pieces.

Results

The blocks slip apart, causing the soil layer to separate.

Why?

Hitting the spoon on the pan causes the blocks to **vibrate** (move back and forth). The spot where earthquake vibrations begin is called the **hypocenter** (point of origin, or **focus**). The trembling produced by the tapping causes the blocks to separate along the diagonal cut. The break in the block represents a **fault** (the break in the earth's crust). The land around a fault shifts due to vibrations produced by earthquakes. It is commonly believed that the **epicenter** (the point on the earth's surface directly above the hypocenter) receives the strongest and the longest shaking from an earthquake. This is not always true. If the break in the crust is at an angle, as in this experiment, then the fault, not the epicenter, is almost always at the center of the largest amount of shaking energy.

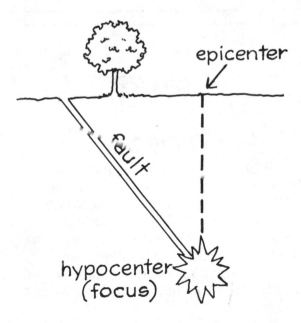

LET'S EXPLORE

1. Would it affect the results if the blocks were tapped along the cut, closer to the top? Repeat the experiment twice, first tapping halfway to the top, and then tapping at a different place along the cut. **Science Fair Hint:** Photographs and/or diagrams of the results can be displayed.

2. How would a vertical cut through the wooden pieces affect the results? Repeat the original experiment using wooden blocks that have vertical edges. **Science Fair Hint:** Use different blocks with vertical and diagonal cuts as part of a project display.

SHOW TIME!

1. A fault can be the result of a diagonal or vertical break in the earth's crust. Two faults representing these types of crustal cleavage are the San Andreas and San Fernando faults. Find out more about these well-known faults. Make and display models representing them. Ask an adult to assist in cutting two empty boxes (use cereal or cake boxes) in half.

- Cut the first box diagonally. Label this as an example of the San Andreas fault.

- Cut the second box vertically. Label this as an example of the San Fernando fault.

2. The three basic types of faults are normal, reverse, and lateral. Clay models similar to the diagram can be constructed and displayed to demonstrate how the blocks of earth on either side of a fault are offset. Research the terms *hanging wall* and *foot wall*, and explain the difference as part of your report.

CHECK IT OUT!

A **fault** is a fracture in the earth's crust whose sides have moved in relation to each other. Find out more about the location of faults and the earthquake activity in these areas.

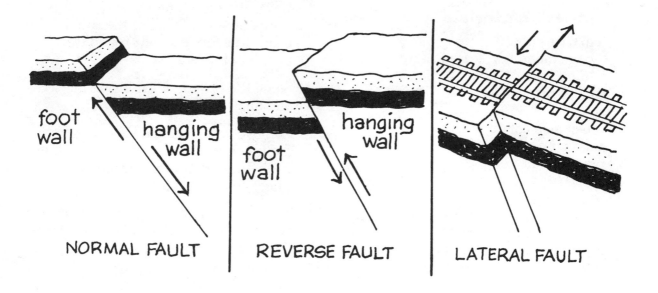

foot wall

hanging wall

NORMAL FAULT

foot wall

hanging wall

REVERSE FAULT

LATERAL FAULT

7

Currents

PROBLEM

How do temperature differences among the earth's layers cause earthquake zones?

Materials

5 to 6 ice cubes
2 large-mouthed, clear-glass, quart (liter) jars
small baby-food jar
spoon
green food coloring
aluminum foil
rubber band
tissue paper
pencil

Procedure

1. Place the ice cubes in the first quart (liter) jar. Fill the jar with cold water.

2. Fill the baby-food jar to overflowing with warm water. Add and stir in six drops of food coloring.

3. Cover the mouth of the baby-food jar with aluminum foil. Use the rubber band to secure the foil around the mouth of the jar.

4. Stand the baby-food jar inside the second quart (liter) jar.

5. Remove any unmelted ice cubes from the first quart (liter) jar, and pour the chilled water into the second quart (liter) so that is filled.

6. Tear three small pieces of tissue paper about as large as the end of your index finger. Lay the three pieces on the surface of the water.

7. Use the pencil to make two small holes in the aluminum foil covering the baby-food jar.

8. Observe the contents of the baby-food jar, as well as the paper pieces on the surface of the water.

Results

The warm, colored water rises out of one of the holes, floats to the surface of the chilled water, and then descends. The paper pieces are moved slightly as the warm water moves along the surface before falling.

Why?

Colored water comes out of only one hole in the foil covering because clear water enters through the second hole at the same time. This exchange of water is due to the difference in their temperatures. Water molecules, like all matter, are spaced closer together when cold and farther apart when heated. The warm, colored water is therefore less dense than the colder clear water. The lighter warm water rises to the top of the heavier chilled water and moves along the surface before cooling and falling. Movement caused by changes in the density of a material is called a **convection current**. The earth has a hot inner core that heats the material above. This hot material, like the warm water, expands and rises toward the earth's crust. Instead of breaking through the crust, it spreads out under the crust—where it cools, contracts, and sinks down again. The hot flowing material from the **mantle** (the second layer of the earth's interior) pushes with great force against the earth's crust. As the current moves it pulls the crust along with it, just as the paper pieces were moved by the flowing hot water. Different currents under the crust pull and push on the earth's crust, causing it to be pulled apart or compressed together where different currents meet. These areas are called **earthquake zones** (areas where earthquakes are most likely to occur) because the pulling or pushing produces **faults** (breaks in the crust). As faults shift, the earth vibrates. These tremblings are called **earthquakes**.

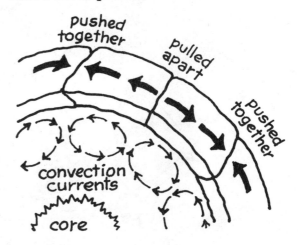

LET'S EXPLORE

1. Would a cool core produce the same crustal movement as a hot core? Repeat the experiment, placing ice-cold water in the baby-food jar and warm water in the area around the baby-food jar. **Science Fair Hint:** Diagrams showing the movement of the colored water, along with diagrams drawn or taken from books showing the convection currents of hot mantle material, can be used as part of a project display.

2. Would more land surface affect the movement of the crust? Repeat the original experiment, placing more pieces of paper on the water's surface.

SHOW TIME!

The forces under the earth's crust that pull the crust apart or push it together can be demonstrated by filling a large container with water. Cut two 2-inch × 4-inch (5-cm × 10-cm) pieces of cardboard. Push the cardboard pieces just below the surface of the water, and ask a helper to sprinkle talcum powder over the surface. Push the cardboard pieces together and observe the folds formed by the powder. Gently pull the cardboard pieces apart, and observe the separation of the powdered surface. Use the results in a project report that describes the movement of mantle material under the earth's crust and its affect on crustal movement and earthquakes.

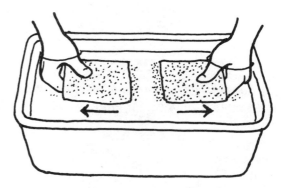

CHECK IT OUT!

In 1928 Arthur Holmes, a British geologist, published an article proposing that convection currents in the earth caused the continents to break apart. This was an interesting idea that eventually led to a new study of the earth called *plate tectonics*. Look for the views of German scientist Alfred Wegener on *continental drift*. What is the difference between plate tectonics and continental drift?

8

Dampers

PROBLEM

How do underground rock formations affect the transmission of earthquake waves?

Materials

scissors
ruler
kite string
3 large metal forks (all the same size)
helper
1 large metal spoon

Procedure

1. Cut two pieces of string, each 2 feet (61 cm) long.

2. Lay the handle of one of the forks in the center of the first piece of string.

3. Tie the string around the fork's han-

dle, making sure that both ends of the string are the same length.

4. Wrap the ends of the string around your left and right index fingers.

5. Place the tip of an index finger lightly in each ear.

6. Lean forward so that the fork hangs freely.

7. Ask a helper to tap the hanging fork with the metal spoon.

8. Repeat the experiment using two forks. (Stack the two forks, and tie the second 2-foot [61-cm] length of string around their handles.)

9. Compare the sound of the single fork to that of the two forks.

Results

The single fork sounds like a church bell, while the two forks have a dull sound.

Why?

The metal in the forks starts to **vibrate** (move back and forth) when struck. When one fork is used, the vibrations travel through the string to the ears. When two forks hang together, they bounce into each other as they move and act like shock absorbers, **dampening** (deadening or stopping) each other's vibrations by soaking up energy from the vibrations. An earthquake is defined as any measurable vibration of the earth's surface. Earthquake vibrations, like the sound from the fork, move outward from the origin of the disturbance, just as waves spread out over water when a rock is dropped in. Underground rock formations affect the **transmission** (sending) of earthquake waves in the same way that the forks affect the transmission of sound vibrations. If the rock formation is **fractured** (cracked), shattered, and broken up, then the rock pieces act like shock absorbers and the wave vibrations die out in short distances. Unbroken rock transmits the **seismic waves** (earthquake vibrations) for long distances.

LET'S EXPLORE

1. Does the number of rock pieces affect the transmission of vibrations? Repeat the experiment using different numbers of forks. **Science Fair Hint:** Display the model used with a description of the sound produced.

2. Does the size of the rock pieces affect the transmission of the vibrations? Repeat the experiment using different sizes of metal spoons, forks, and knives. **Science Fair Hint:** Display the model used with a description of the sound produced. A drawing of broken **bedrock** (a rock formation under the ground) can be used to compare the transmission of sound through the separate metal pieces to the transmission of seismic waves through broken rock pieces.

SHOW TIME!

To demonstrate the effects of localized seismic shocks in broken bedrock, toss a baseball onto a feather pillow. To demonstrate the transmission of earthquake vibrations through unbroken rock structures, drop the ball onto a drum or the bottom of a metal baking pan. Photographs taken while performing the different experiments can be used as part of a project display. Include descriptions of what happens during each procedure.

CHECK IT OUT!

One of the most powerful seismic disturbances in U.S. history occurred in New Madrid, Missouri, in the winter of 1811–1812. A series of tremendous earthquakes shook half the continent. A quake of equal magnitude hit San Francisco in 1906, but the tremors were not as far-reaching as were those of the New Madrid quake. The underlying rock formations of the land west of the Rocky Mountains are more broken than they are to the east of the Rockies. Find out more about the effects of these two quakes as well as other quakes. Compare the damage done by quakes of equal magnitude that have occurred to the west and to the east of the Rocky Mountains.

9

S–Waves

PROBLEM

What are S-waves, and how do they move through the earth's interior?

Materials

6-foot (2-m) rope

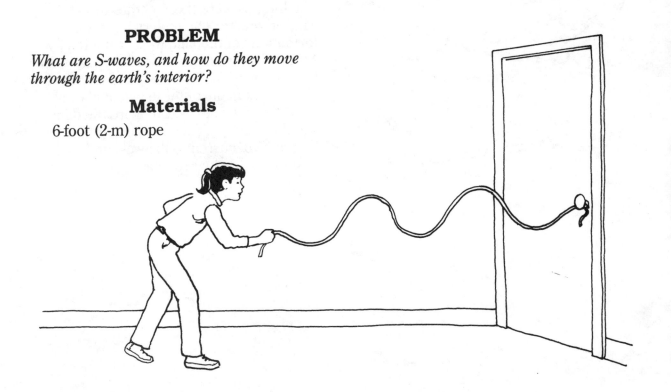

Procedure

1. Tie one end of the rope to a door knob.

2. Hold the free end of the rope in your hand.

3. Back away from the door until the rope is straight.

4. Gently shake the rope up and down.

5. Gently shake the rope from side to side.

Results

Vertical and horizontal S-shaped waves form along the length of the rope.

Why?

The shaking of the earth caused by sudden movement of rock beneath the surface is called an earthquake. This movement within the earth produces **seismic waves** (earthquake vibrations) that move through the body of the earth toward its surface. These seismic waves inside the earth are called **body waves**. The most energetic and fastest body waves are **P-waves** (primary waves).

S-waves (secondary waves) are slower body waves that travel beneath the earth's surface, and arrive five to seven minutes after P-waves. Energy from S-waves moves away from the source of vibrations, causing the rock layers to ripple in the same way that the ripples moved along the rope. This up-and-down or side-to-side motion is called a **transverse wave**.

LET'S EXPLORE

1. Does the energy of the earthquake affect the **amplitude** (height) of S-waves? Repeat the experiment, shaking the rope vigorously. **Science Fair Hint:** Record the results, and make sketches of the difference in the amplitude of the waves, as part of a project display.

2. Would the distance away from the **hypocenter** (the place where vibrations begin within the earth) affect the amplitude (height) of S-waves? Repeat the experiment twice, first using a shorter section of rope, and then using a longer rope. Be sure to shake the rope with the same amount of force with each testing.

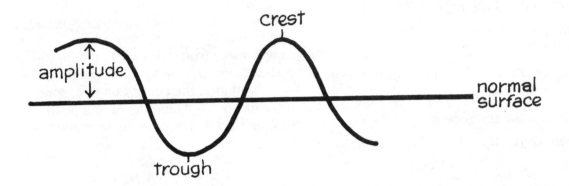

amplitude

crest

normal surface

trough

SHOW TIME!

1. Display pictures from books and/or make diagrams showing S-shaped waves. Label these parts of the S-wave:

   - *crest* (highest part of the wave).

   - *trough* (lowest part of the wave).

   - *amplitude* (height of the wave from normal ground position).

2. Construct an "earthquake box" to demonstrate the affect of the up-and-down or side-to-side movement of S-waves on the earth's surface. Cut a 6-inch × 2-inch (15-cm × 5-cm) section from the bottom of a shoe box. Insert one paper brad (round paper fastener), on each side of the two short sides of the opening. Attach a rubber band around the brads so that it stretches across the opening. Cut a hole in the side of the box large enough to insert your hand. Cut a strip of paper 4 inches × 6 inches (10 cm × 15 cm). Lay the paper over the rubber band. Pull the ends of the paper under the box, and attach the ends to the underside with tape. Tie a string to the center of one side of the rubber band. Set the box on a sturdy table, and cover the paper with a layer of table salt. Hold the box with one hand to support it

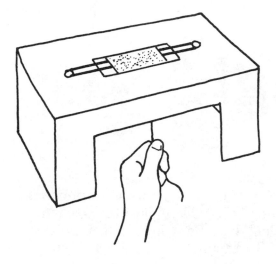

while pulling the string to the side. Release the string to produce horizontal movement. Pull the string down about 2 inches (5 cm), and release it to allow for up-and-down motion. Describe the movement of the salt crystals lying on the paper. The earthquake box can be part of the project display and could be used to demonstrate the different motion of S-waves when giving an oral presentation.

CHECK IT OUT!

Find out about the different types of seismic waves and the materials that they can travel through. Look for information about how scientists use the ability of seismic waves to travel through different types of materials in order to determine the content of the earth's interior. Information can be found on page 80 of *Earth Science for Every Kid* (New York: Wiley, 1991, by Janice VanCleave).

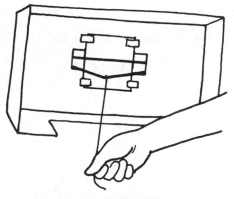

UNDERSIDE

10

Bang!

PROBLEM

How is the energy of seismic P-waves transmitted through the earth?

Materials

scissors
ruler
string
masking tape
5 marbles

Procedure

1. Cut five separate pieces of string, each 12 inches (30 cm) long.

2. Tape one piece of string to each of the marbles.

3. Tape the free end of each string to the edge of a table. Adjust the position and length of the strings so that the marbles are the same height and are touching each other.

4. Pull one of the end marbles to the side, and then release it.

5. Observe any movement of the marbles.

Results

The marble swings down, striking the closest marble in its path, and stops moving. The marble on the opposite end swings outward, and strikes its closest neighboring marble when it swings back into its original position. The cycle of the end marbles swinging back and forth continues for a few seconds.

Why?

Raising the end marble gives it energy, which is transferred to the marble it strikes. This energy is passed from one marble to the next, as each marble pushes against the marble in front of it. The end marble is pushed away from the group. The transfer of energy from one marble to the next simulates the movement of energy from the blow of a seismic P-wave (primary earthquake wave) as it travels through the earth's interior. The first sign that an earthquake has occurred is the hammerlike blow felt and heard as a P-wave exits through the earth's surface. Before that, P-waves move through liquids and solids by **compressing** (pushing together) the material directly in front of them. Each compressed particle quickly springs back to its original position as soon as the energy moves on. The **crust** (outer layer) of the earth moves upward as it is hit with the energy of the P-wave, and then settles back into place when the energy moves on.

LET'S EXPLORE

1. Would it affect the transmission of energy if the marbles were not in line? Stick pieces of clay on the side of the table in order to change the position of the marbles. Be sure that the marbles touch at some point, but that all of the marbles are at different heights.

2. Would changing the distance between molecules affect the transfer of energy? Repeat the original experiment, moving the pieces of tape supporting the marbles farther apart, so that there is a slight separation between each marble.

SHOW TIME!

1. Use a Slinky™ to demonstrate the particle movement of a seismic P-wave as it moves from the **focus** (starting point) of an earthquake to the **epicenter** (the point on the earth's surface directly above the focus). The Slinky can be used as part of a project presentation by slightly stretching it vertically, and attaching its top and bottom loops to the display. Squeeze four to five loops together at one end, and release.

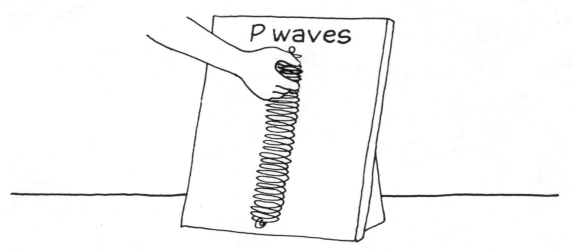

2. Seismic waves move more slowly through sand because the energy of the waves moves forward in different directions as the sand particles move outward in all directions. To demonstrate this, cover the end of a paper tube with a paper towel. Secure the paper towel to the tube with a rubber band. Fill the tube with dry rice. Use your fingers to push down on the rice. Try to push the rice down and out through the paper towel.

CHECK IT OUT!

P-waves are the swiftest seismic waves. Find out the speed of P-waves as they travel through the different layers of the earth's interior: crust, mantle, and core. You could display a diagram of a cross section of the earth, with speeds of a P-wave indicated on each layer.

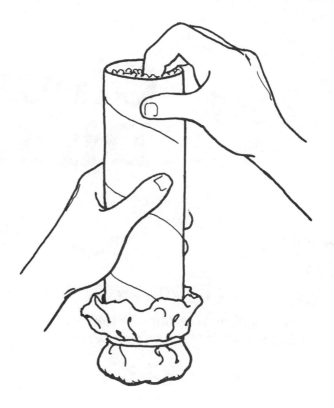

Change of Direction

PROBLEM

What happens to earthquake wave energy when it reaches the earth's surface?

Materials

scissors
ruler
sewing elastic, ½ inch (1.25 cm) wide
marking pen
12 drinking straws
stapler
masking tape

Procedure

1. Cut a 3-foot (1-m) strip of elastic.

2. Starting 6 inches (15 cm) from one end of the elastic strip, use the marking pen to make 12 marks, one every 2 inches (4 cm) on the strip.

3. Place one straw under each mark, and staple the elastic to the center of each straw.

4. Tape one end of the elastic to the top of a door frame, so that the elastic hangs freely in the doorway.

5. Hold the bottom of the elastic strip in your hand, and pull it downward about 12 inches (30 cm).

6. Twist the bottom straw around for one half turn, and then release.

7. Observe the motions of all the straws.

Results

Starting from the bottom, each straw twists in turn until the top is reached and then the motion moves down the strip. This wavelike motion continues for a few seconds, and then the straws return to their original position.

Why?

Rocks within the earth's crust are squeezed, pulled, pushed, and twisted by such forces as the movement of hot materials beneath the crust, the earth's rotation, gravity of the sun and moon, and the earth's own gravity. Earthquakes start when enough force causes rocks to break and move apart. Twisting the bottom straw out of position can be compared to the strain placed on rocks within the earth's crust. Releasing the straw sends a wave of energy up through the elastic. The energy moves along from one straw to the next, twisting each straw out of place.

In a like manner, to get to the earth's surface the energy from an earthquake twists rock structures out of place. The rock structures return to their original position as the energy moves toward the earth's surface. When the energy in your experiment reaches the top of the elastic strip, most of it has no place to go but back down the strip. The wave of motion of the straws continues as the energy moves up and down the strip until the energy is used up. All of the seismic energy, however, is not **reflected** (bounced back) into the earth; some moves along the surface, producing wavelike motion as the energy passes through the outer layer of the earth.

LET'S EXPLORE

1. Would a less **flexible** (able to bend or stretch without breaking) material affect the transmission of energy? Repeat the experiment using tape instead of the elastic strip. A piece of tape on the front and back of the straws prevents the straws from pulling free.

2. How would a more solid structure behave if twisted? Repeat the original experiment using a single piece of cardboard about 24 inches (60 cm) long and as wide as a straw, instead of separate straws. **Science Fair Hint:** Display the model from this experiment and from the other experiments. As part of an oral presentation, demonstrate the wave motion produced by each model.

SHOW TIME!

Waves that move along the earth's surface cause the land to move up and down. These waves, called **Raleigh waves**, behave much like water waves. Fill a large bowl with water. Tap the surface of the water with the end of a pencil to demonstrate the appearance of Raleigh surface waves. Diagrams can be used to represent these surface waves.

CHECK IT OUT!

The seismic energy that moves along the surface of the earth produces two types of motion:

- **Raleigh waves**, which move up and down.

- **Love waves**, which move back and forth.

Find out more about these two types of surface waves. The difference in the damage caused by the waves, as well as information about the scientists who first identified these two different movements, can be part of a project report.

12

Interior

PROBLEM

How are seismic waves used to determine that the earth's interior has different layers?

Materials

scissors
rulers
duct tape
large cooking pot
10 coins
helper

Procedure

1. Cut a 2-inch × 2-inch (5-cm × 5-cm) square piece of tape.

2. Center the piece of tape inside the bottom of the pot.

3. Set the pot on a table.

4. Hold one coin between the fingers of one hand.

5. Rest the hand holding the coin over the edge of the pot.

6. Try to drop the coin onto the piece of tape.

7. Adjust the position of your hand until coins can be dropped onto the piece of tape.

8. Keep your hand in place while a helper first removes the coins and then fills the pot with about 4 inches (10 cm) of water.

9. Drop the coins, one at a time, into the water.

Results

The coins drop straight down onto the piece of tape when falling through the air, but change direction when they hit the water's surface.

Why?

The path of the coins **refracts** (changes direction) when moving from the air into the water. The change of direction occurs at the boundary between the air and the water. Abrupt changes in the path of the coins indicate a change in the **density** (the number of molecules in a specific volume) through which the coin moves. **Seismic waves** (earthquake vibrations) would travel in a straight path if the interior materials of the earth were all of the same density. **Seismologists** (scientists who study earthquakes) observe that the paths of these energy waves, like those of the coins, change directions. It has been concluded that the waves become refracted at boundaries between materials of different densities. This gives clues to the position of different layers of material within the earth.

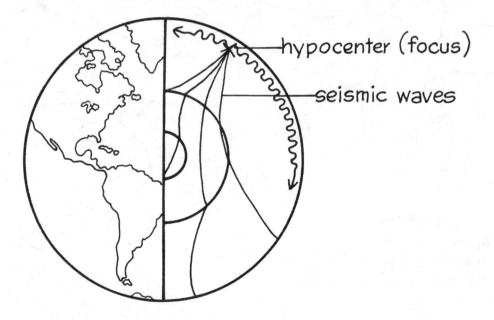

hypocenter (focus)

seismic waves

LET'S EXPLORE

1. Would a different-sized coin better demonstrate refraction? Repeat the experiment twice, first using a smaller coin, then using a larger coin. **Science Fair Hint:** Determine which coin refracts the most, and use this coin during a presentation of the project experiment.

2. Does the depth of the water affect the amount that the path of the coin is refracted? Repeat the original experiment twice, first decreasing the depth of the water, and then increasing the depth of the water.

SHOW TIME!

The path of the coins, as well as that of earthquake energy waves, is most refracted (bent) when moving from one substance into a new substance of a different density. To demonstrate this, fill a clear plastic drinking glass one-fourth full with clear corn syrup. Slowly pour water into the glass until it is three-fourths full. Drop a coin from a height slightly above the surface of the water, and observe its path through the liquids. Use the container as part of a project display.

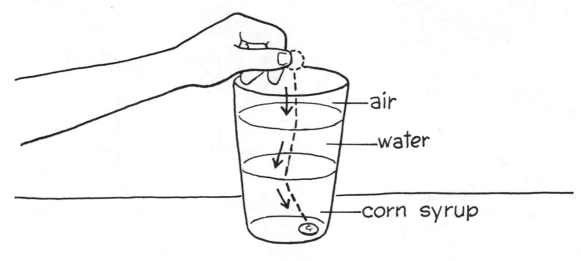

13

Recorder

PROBLEM

How does a seismograph record the magnitude of an earthquake?

Materials

adult helper
cardboard box, measuring about 12
    inches (30 cm) on each side
scissors
ruler
adding-machine paper
string
pencil
5-oz (150-ml) paper cup
masking tape
black marking pen
5-oz (150-ml) cup of small rocks
modeling clay

Procedure

CAUTION: Ask an adult to cut the holes in the box.

1. Turn the box on its side with the opening facing outward.

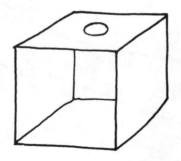

2. Cut a 2-inch (4-cm) diameter circle in the center of the top side of the box.

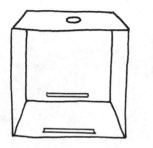

3. Cut two ½-inch × 4-inch (1-cm × 8-cm) slits in the box. The first slit should be in the center of the bottom, near the edge. The second slit must be in line with the first slit, in the back side of the box.

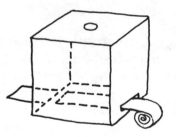

4. Cut a 2-foot (60-cm) length of adding-machine paper.

5. Thread the strip of paper through the slits in the box, so that about 2 inches (4 cm) extends past the front edge of the box.

6. Cut two 24-inch (60-cm) lengths of string.

7. Use the point of a pencil to punch two holes below the rim of the cup, one on each side of the cup.

8. Tie one string in each hole.

9. Push the free ends of the string through the hole in the top of the box.

10. Tape the ends of the string to the pencil, and lay the pencil across the hole.

11. Push the tip of the marking pen through the bottom of the paper cup.

12. Fill the cup with small rocks.

13. Wind the string around the pencil until the tip of the pen barely touches the adding-machine paper beneath it.

14. Use modeling clay to secure the pencil and to prevent the string from unwinding.

15. Pull the adding-machine paper forward with one hand, and gently shake the box with your other hand.

16. Observe the markings made by the pen on the paper.

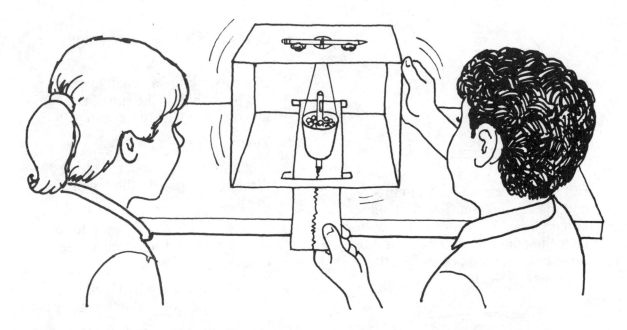

Results

The pen draws a zigzag line on the paper as the paper moves underneath the pen.

Why?

The **inertia** (resistance to a change in motion) of the heavy cup keeps it steady while the box shakes back and forth. As the box shakes, it moves the paper from side to side underneath the pen; thus, a zigzag line is drawn as the paper is pulled forward. A **seismograph** (an instrument used to measure the shaking energy of an earthquake) uses a very heavy suspended object that remains steady, while the frame to which it is attached moves when the earth vibrates. A recording pen attached to the suspended object records the vibrations on the moving paper. The width of the zigzag produced increases with the **magnitude** (measurement of the amount of shaking energy released) of the earthquake being recorded. The written record is called a **seismogram**.

LET'S EXPLORE

1. Does the weight of the cup affect the seismogram produced? Empty the cup and repeat the experiment.

2. Does the direction of the earthquake affect the pattern on the seismogram? Use a compass to position the box so that the tape points in a north-to-south direction. Repeat the experiment, tapping the box from the four different directions—north, east, south, and west. Label each seismogram with the direction of the vibrations.

SHOW TIME!

You can construct a sensitive seismograph using a beam of light. Place a bowl full of water on a table. Ask a helper to hold a flashlight so that its beam of light falls on the surface of the water and is reflected to a nearby wall. Watch the spot of light on the wall while you gently tap the surface of the water with your finger. Produce other small quakes by clapping your hands together or hitting the table. This model can be used as part of a project display.

CHECK IT OUT!

Andrija Mohorovicic, a Yugoslavian seismologist, analyzed the **seismograms** (zigzag lines recorded on paper by a **seismograph**—a machine that measures seismic waves) of a Balkan earthquake in 1909. Read about this scientist, and think about these questions:

- What did he discover from the seismograms about the speed of seismic waves at depths around 25 miles (40 km)?

- What is *Moho* short for?

14

One More?

PROBLEM

How much shaking energy does a Richter-scale measurement (a method of measuring earthquake energy) represent?

Materials

open cardboard box measuring about 18 inches × 12 inches × 6 inches (45 cm × 30 cm × 15 cm)
popped popcorn
yardstick (meterstick)

Procedure

1. Cover the bottom of the cardboard box with popcorn. *NOTE: The size of the box can vary without changing the results.*

2. Raise the box 1 inch (2.5 cm) above the floor.

3. Drop the box.

4. Observe any movement of the popcorn kernels inside the box.

5. Raise the box 32 inches (80 cm) above the floor.

6. Drop the box.

7. Observe any movement of the popcorn kernels inside the box.

Results

The popcorn kernels inside the box are shaken when the box strikes the floor. The kernels move upward slightly when the box is dropped from a height of 1 inch (2.5 cm), and fly out of the box when it is dropped from a height of 32 inches (80 cm).

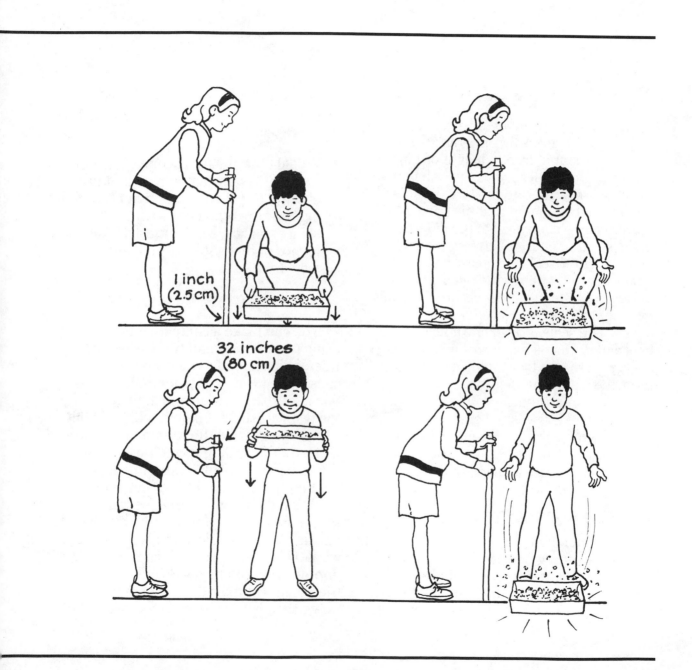

1 inch
(2.5 cm)

32 inches
(80 cm)

Why?

The energy stored by raising the box 32 inches (80 cm) is 32 times as great as the energy stored from a height of 1 inch (2.5 cm). Once released, energy shakes the popcorn kernels in the box. The difference in the amount that the popcorn moves can be compared to the difference in the shaking energy between numbers on the Richter scale for measuring earthquake energy. The **Richter scale** is a number system used to measure the total magnitude (energy released) of an earthquake. The scale is a set of whole numbers and decimals between 1 and 9. The energy increases by a multiple of 32 times from one whole number to the next. For example, an earthquake with a Richter magnitude of 7 releases 32 times as much energy as one with a magnitude of 6, and 1,026 (32×32) times as much energy as an earthquake with a magnitude of 5.

LET'S EXPLORE

1. How much difference is there in the shaking energy of less than one whole-number Richter-scale measurement? Drop the box from different heights between 1 inch (2.5 cm) and 32 inches (80 cm). Compare the distance the kernels move with each height the box is dropped.

2. Would other materials move differently with the same amount of shaking energy? Repeat the experiment, replacing the popcorn kernels with such substances as salt, sand, or gravel. Keep a record of the results of all materials tested.

SHOW TIME!

You can make a comparison of energy using two marbles and two yardsticks (metersticks), and a ruler. For best results, lay a towel on a smooth floor. Position a marble between and at the end of the two yardsticks (metersticks) laid out on the towel. Hold the ruler at an angle so that a marble rolling down it will strike the stationary marble. Experiment with the height of the incline so that at one elevation the rolling marble sends the stationary marble forward 1 inch (2.5 cm), and at the second elevation sends it forward 32 inches (80 cm). Diagrams and/or photographs can be displayed comparing the heights of the rulers. It should be noted that the two heights represent the difference in the energy between each whole-number Richter-scale measurement.

CHECK IT OUT!

It is commonly believed that many small quakes in one area release energy, and thus reduce the possibility of a large shock in the future. A comparison of Richter magnitudes for measured earthquakes can be used to show that this idea is physically impossible. An example would be: The 1971 San Francisco quake had a magnitude of 6.5, and the 1964 Alaska quake was measured at 8.5. There is a difference of two Richter scale divisions between these quakes. The shaking energy of the earthquake with the higher magnitude was 32×32—or 1,024—times as great. This means that it would take 1,024 San Francisco quakes (magnitude 6.5) to equal the energy of the Alaska earthquake (magnitude 8.5).

15

How Strong?

PROBLEM

How does the distance of the earth's surface from the epicenter affect the intensity of an earthquake?

Materials

cardboard box (the bottom side should be about 18 inches [45 cm] long and 12 inches [30 cm] wide)
box of dominoes

Procedure

1. Turn the box upside down on a flat surface such as a floor.

2. Build two "domino houses" on the surface of the upturned box, the first 4 inches (10 cm) from one edge of the box, and the second 4 inches (10 cm) from the opposite edge of the box. To build each house:

   • Stand four dominoes on end adjacent to each other to form four outside walls.

   • Place one domino across the top for the roof.

3. In front of one of the domino houses, gently tap the box ten times with your fingers.

4. Observe the movement of both domino houses.

Results

The tapping causes the dominoes that make up the houses to move out of position. The house closer to the tapped area is more damaged than the house farther from the tapped area.

Why?

Tapping the box sends out waves of vibrating energy across the top of the box. The energy weakens as it travels outward. The dominoes in the house closer to the tapped area are moved more because they received the greatest amount of vibrating energy. The intensity of earthquakes is *usually* greatest near the initial source of vibrations. This is not *always* true, because earthquake **intensity** is a measure of all the damage done by the earthquake: the effects on the land, the extent to which buildings are deformed, the number of people killed or injured, and many other changes.

The distance from the source of vibration does affect the intensity of an earthquake, but intensity is also affected by other factors, such as the nature of the ground and the stability of the structures. The shocks from an earthquake whose source is at sea could damage the land many miles away. In this case, the intensity is greatest at the farther distance from the vibrating source.

LET'S EXPLORE

1. Does the building structure affect the intensity of an earthquake? Repeat the experiment using different structures to represent types of buildings. Some of the structures, such as a house of cards, should represent houses with minimum frame strength. Other structures, such as a cardboard container, could represent a house with its frame strongly held together. **Science Fair**

Hint: Use the structures as part of a project display. Indicate which structure would contribute to a higher-intensity measurement during an earthquake.

2. How does the earth's crust affect the intensity of an earthquake? Repeat the experiment, placing the structures on different surfaces. Examples might be the bottom of a metal pan, or a tray filled with dry uncooked rice. **Science Fair Hint:** Photographs and/or diagrams representing the surfaces tested, along with the results, can be displayed.

SHOW TIME!

1. A sinkhole would greatly increase the intensity of an earthquake. **Sinkholes** are underground cavities dissolved in limestone rock. **Seismic waves** (earthquake vibrations) could cause these cavities to collapse, forming a hole that swallows up everything sitting atop it. Build and display a sinkhole model. Remove the cardboard strip to demonstrate the collapse of the cavity.

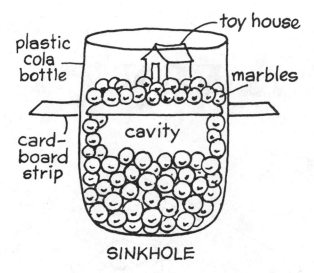

plastic
cola
bottle

toy house

marbles

card-
board
strip

cavity

SINKHOLE

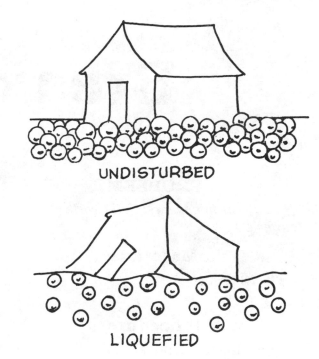

UNDISTURBED

LIQUEFIED

2. Earthquakes can cause **landfills** (land that had been built up by adding dirt, rocks, garbage, or other fillers) to be changed from relatively firm ground into something that behaves like a liquid. Use diagrams to represent the transformation. Before the earthquake, the grains of undisturbed soil stack on top of each other, making it possible for the soil to support the weight of buildings. The vibrations cause water in the soil to push the grains out of place, weakening the supporting power of the liquefied soil.

CHECK IT OUT!

The Richter scale measures the shaking energy of an earthquake, while the Mercali scale measures intensity: the damage done to the land, people, and structures. Read about this twelve-point scale and make a list of each intensity level to be used as part of a project display.

16

Break Away

PROBLEM

How do earthquakes crack the earth's surface?

Materials

facial tissue
ruler

Procedure

1. Fold the tissue in half.

2. Hold the ends of the tissue in your hands.

3. Measure the length of the folded side of the tissue.

4. Gently pull outward on both ends of the tissue without breaking it, and then release.

5. Measure the length of the folded side of the tissue again.

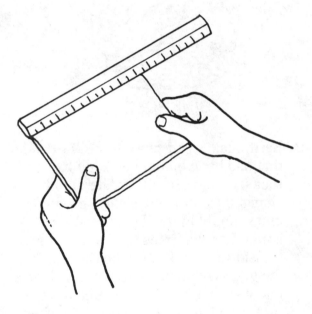

6. Slowly pull outward on both ends of the tissue until it breaks.

7. Observe the movement of the tissue.

Results

The tissue stretches slightly, but returns to its original length when released. Excessive pulling on the paper causes it to break apart. At the moment the paper splits, your hands quickly move apart, further separating the two sections of tissue held in each hand.

Why?

The elastic property of the tissue allows it to be stretched and then return to its original shape. All solids, even rocks, stretch when a force is applied, and many are able to return to their original shape when the force is removed. The outward push or pulling force on any solid is called a **tension force**. Solids have a limit to their elasticity, and if pushed past this limit, they break. The tissue broke when stretched past its **elastic limit**. Tension forces can also stretch rocks past their elastic limit, causing the earth to split. The vibrating energy from an earthquake produces forces that can cause sections of the earth's **crust** (the solid upper layer) to split apart. The elastic limit of the rock layer affects the damage done by **seismic** (earthquake) vibrations.

LET'S EXPLORE

1. Does the direction the tissue is folded affect the results? Repeat the experiment, folding the tissue from different sides including diagonally.

2. Would the type of paper affect the results? Repeat the experiment using different samples of paper, such as typing paper, newspaper, and paper towels. **Science Fair Hint:** As part of your project, display pictures of land areas split apart by earthquakes.

SHOW TIME!

1. Some of the worst damage during an earthquake results from forces that twist and tear rock layers apart. These twisting forces are called **shear forces**, and can be demonstrated by placing your thumbs close together on the tissue and twisting. Display photographs of the tissues before and after the twisting to demonstrate the tearing effect of shearing forces.

2. Test the elasticity of different materials, such as a pencil, a stick, a cracker, or a cookie. Grasp the ends of each object. Push down on the ends with your hands until the object breaks. Compare the amount of force required to break each material. Display photographs to represent the procedure and materials tested.

CHECK IT OUT!

Earthquakes cause the earth's surface to be pushed together, pulled apart, and twisted. These movements are respectively caused by compression, tension, and shear forces. Find out more about the surface movement created by these forces. Display diagrams representing the damaging results of each. Pictures of forces acting in the earth's crust can be found in earth science textbooks.

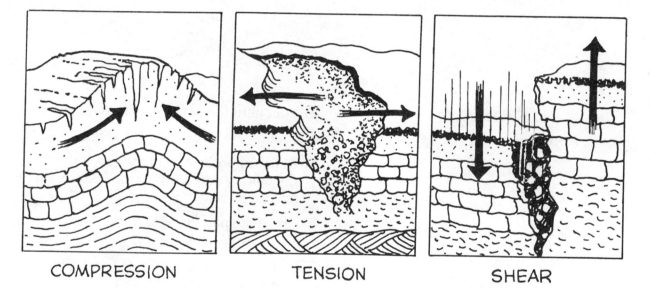

COMPRESSION TENSION SHEAR

Megawaves

PROBLEM

How do earthquakes affect sea water?

Materials

modeling clay
yardstick (meterstick)
bathtub
8-inch × 12-inch (20 cm × 30 cm)
   baking pan, with lid

Procedure

1. Use a piece of modeling clay to stand the yardstick (meterstick) at one end of a bathtub. Be sure the largest number is at the top of the stick.

2. Fill the tub with about 4 inches (10 cm) of water.

3. Wait until the water's surface is calm.

4. Secure the lid on the baking pan.

5. At the opposite end of the tub, push the baking pan down to the bottom, and then raise it quickly.

6. Move the pan up and down in the water three times.

7. Observe the movement of the water around the measuring stick.

Results

Waves move quickly toward the measuring stick. The water rises above, then sinks below, the normal 4-inch (10-cm) level.

Why?

The up-and-down movement of the pan causes the water to rise and fall with the pan. The energy of the moving water is transferred from one water molecule to the next, sending waves across the surface of the water. **Seismic waves** (earthquake vibrations) can cause pieces of rock on the bottom of the sea to move. When the motion of the rock is **vertical** (up and down), the movement is called dip-slip displacement, and the water above the rocks rises and falls with the moving sea bed.

This dip-slip displacement causes the water first to withdraw, and then rush back as giant waves that appear as a solid wall of water, moving up to 500 miles per hour (800 km/hr) and reaching terrifying heights. In the ocean there may be a calm period of 15 to 45 minutes between these monstrous waves. These megawaves are often incorrectly called **tidal waves**, but their correct name is **seismic sea waves**. The Japanese name for the waves is **tsunamis**, a name that has been widely adopted by **seismologists** (scientists who study earthquakes).

LET'S EXPLORE

1. How does the speed of the dip-slip displacement of rocks affect the water? Repeat the experiment twice, first moving the pan very slowly in an up-and-down direction, and then moving it quickly. Observe and record the changes in the height of the water with each trial.

2. Does the shape of the shoreline affect the height of the waves? Repeat the original experiment using bricks to narrow the passage of the water at the end closer to the measuring stick. Place a towel on the bottom of the tub to protect it from being scratched, and then stack bricks on both sides of the tub. Change the number of bricks, and observe and record the height of the waves that strike the measuring stick. **Science Fair Hint:** Diagrams showing the height of the waves produced in each experiment can be used as part of a project display.

SHOW TIME!

Fill an outdoor wading pool with about 2 inches (5 cm) of water. Place two bricks end to end at the edge of the pool. Place a flat board or pan in front of the bricks. Generate waves by pushing the board down into the water, and then allowing the board to come back up. Repeat so that a series of waves moves toward the bricks. Place the bricks in a "V" shape,

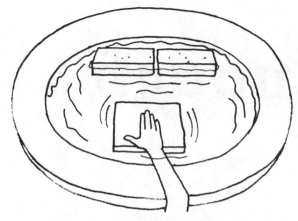

MODEL OF A SHORELINE

MODEL OF AN INLET

but have both ends of the "V" open. Generate a series of waves with the board again. Show photographs of this experiment to go along with a description of how waves are affected as they travel through inlets or bays as compared to shorelines.

CHECK IT OUT!

Some of the world's greatest disasters have resulted from severe earthquakes. A quake in Lisbon, Portugal, on November 1, 1755, flattened most of the houses in the city and produced a tremendous tsunami. Write a report about this and other earthquakes that produced tsunamis. A map showing the location of deadly tsunamis and their dates can be displayed.

 **18**

Long Enough

PROBLEM
What effect does the duration of an earthquake have on the land surface?

Materials
large shoe box
unpopped kernels of popcorn
timer
metal spoon

Procedure
1. Turn the box upside down on top of a table.
2. Cover the roof the inverted box with a layer of popcorn kernels.
3. Hold the box steady with one hand.
4. Set the timer for 5 seconds.
5. Immediately start gently tapping the spoon on the side of the box just below the top edge.
6. Observe the movement of the kernels as you tap.
7. Stop tapping at the end of 5 seconds.
8. Set the timer for 10 seconds, and repeat the experiment.
9. Observe the movement of the kernels again as you gently tap the side of the box.

Results

Tapping the box causes the popcorn kernels to vibrate (move back and forth). Those kernels near the edge fall off the box, while the ones farther from the edge move only slightly. Increasing the time duration of the tapping causes more kernels to move farther away from their original position.

Why?

The longer the duration of an earthquake, the greater is the total amount of energy received by the affected area, which results in more damage. The duration of an earthquake is related to the amount of shaking energy released by the quake. Shaking energy is referred to as the magnitude of the earthquake and is measured by the **Richter scale** which ranges from 1 to 9. There is no absolute time of duration for earthquakes, but, generally, quakes with moderate shaking energy (magnitude up to 6) last from 5 to 10 seconds. Major quakes (magnitude of 6.5 to 7.5) last 15 to 30 seconds, while great quakes (magnitude of 7.75 or more) last for 30 to 60 seconds.

LET'S EXPLORE

1. Gentle tapping for 5 to 10 seconds represents the magnitude and duration of a moderate earthquake. Represent a major earthquake by repeating the experiment twice, first tapping harder for 15 seconds, and then tapping even harder for 30 seconds. **Science Fair Hint:** Compare the number of popcorn kernels that fall off the box with the different magnitudes and time durations.

2. How would a different ground cover be affected by the vibrations? Cover the box with dirt, and repeat the experiment. (Perform the experiment outside, or use a tray to collect falling dirt.) **Science Fair Hint:** Pictures of the surface of the box before and after tapping on the box's side can be used as part of a science fair display. Label each diagram with the time in order of least to greatest duration.

SHOW TIME!

How are structures affected by the duration of an earthquake? Use dominoes or wooden blocks to construct "houses" about 12 inches (30 cm) from the edge of a table. (Experiment 15 gives instructions for building domino houses.) Use your fist to gently hit the edge of the table nearest the houses for 10 seconds. Observe any changes in the structures of the houses. Repair any damage to the houses, and then repeat by hitting the table with the same force for 30 seconds. Use photographs of the houses, before and after vibrating the table, as part of your project display.

CHECK IT OUT!

Earthquakes usually last for a short duration of from 10 to 60 seconds. Read about different recorded earthquakes, and make a chart dividing them into categories of great, major, and moderate quakes.

19

Side-to-Side

PROBLEM

How do buildings respond to lateral (side-to-side) movements produced by earthquakes?

Materials

1 sheet of coarse (rough) sandpaper
Slinky™

Procedure

1. Place the sandpaper on a table.

2. Stand the Slinky on end on the sandpaper.

3. Grab the edge of the sandpaper with your fingers, and quickly pull the paper forward about 6 inches (15 cm).

4. Observe the movement of the Slinky.

Results

The bottom of the Slinky is pulled to the side. The top section of the Slinky temporarily lags behind, and then springs back into place.

Why?

The bottom of the coil is pulled to the side by the movement of the paper beneath it. A similar movement occurs during an earthquake, when the ground below a building moves **laterally** (sideways). These lateral movements are very destructive, since they cause the walls to bend to one side. **Inertia** (the tendency of an object at rest to remain at rest) holds the upper part of the coil or a building in a leaning position for a fraction of a second, and then the structures snap back into their original shapes. During a typical

earthquake lasting only 15 seconds, a
building may bend and snap between 15
and 100 times, depending on its structure.

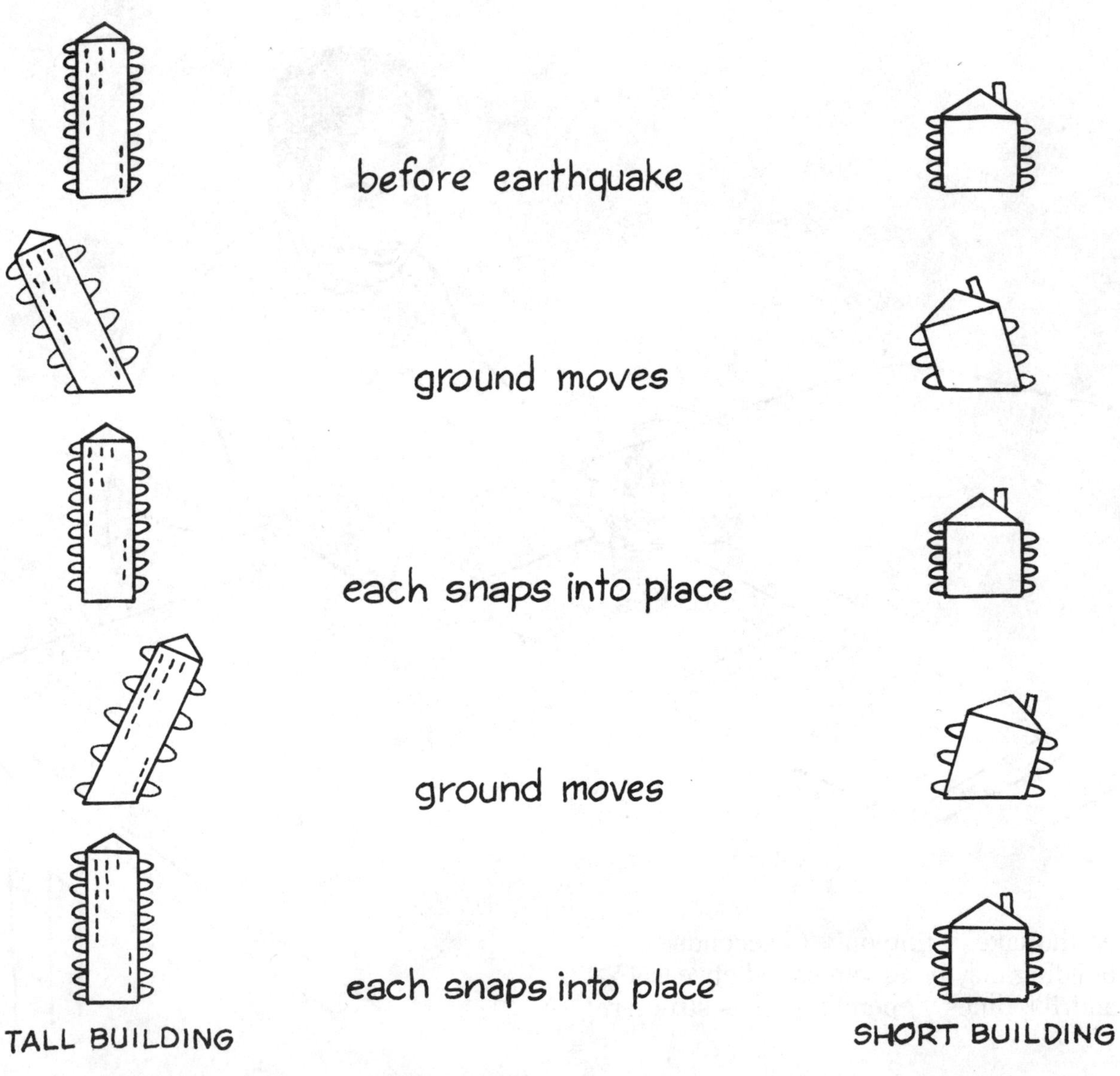

before earthquake

ground moves

each snaps into place

ground moves

each snaps into place

TALL BUILDING

SHORT BUILDING

LET'S EXPLORE

1. Earthquakes do not wait for one wave of energy to make a complete ground-to-roof-to-ground cycle before the next wave of energy enters the building. What would happen if the Slinky received energy waves from different directions? Repeat the experiment, but jerk the paper back and forth. **Science Fair Hint:** Use diagrams and/or photographs along with a written description of the results as part of a science fair project.

2. Would a taller building be more affected? Repeat the experiment using a longer coil (connect two Slinkys). **Science Fair Hint:** Tape a paper representation of a skyscraper to the Slinky. Display the model and photographs or diagrams indicating the changes to the building during and after the seismic (earthquake) tremors.

SHOW TIME!

Demonstrate inertia by placing the end of a 2-inch × 12-inch (5-cm × 30-cm) strip of wax paper under a glass of water. Hold the free end of the strip in your hand, and pull the paper out from under the glass with a quick, straight , forceful movement. *NOTE: This may take a little practice, so be sure to place the glass about 6 inches (15 cm) from the edge of the table to prevent it from falling off. If you pull too slowly, the glass moves forward.*

CHECK IT OUT!

Find out more about the erratic movement of structures such as buildings or bridges during an earthquake.

20

Flexible

PROBLEM

How do earthquakes affect unbraced frame structures?

Materials

masking tape
drinking straws
typing paper
marking pen
helper

Procedure

1. Tape four straws together to form the outline of a square form.

2. Lay the sheet of typing paper on a table.

3. Position the straw frame on the lower right-hand corner of the sheet of paper.

4. Use the marking pen to draw around the outside of the square frame.

5. Hold the bottom straw firmly against the paper with your left hand.

6. Use your right hand to push the top straw as far to the left as possible without breaking the frame.

7. Hold the frame in this leaning position while a helper marks around the outside of the frame.

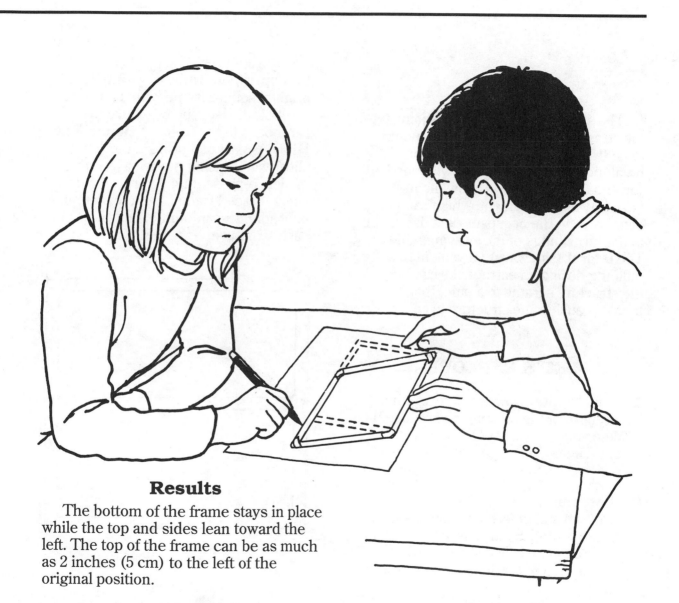

Results

The bottom of the frame stays in place while the top and sides lean toward the left. The top of the frame can be as much as 2 inches (5 cm) to the left of the original position.

Why?

The straw, as well as the tape joining the straws together, allows the structure to be **flexible** (able to bend without breaking). Frame structures with **vertical** (up-and-down) supports allow the most flexibility and movement, which can be dangerous to the occupants and damaging to the furnishings of the swaying building. The **lateral** (sideways) movement of a building during an earthquake can bend the structure's frame to a point that it breaks, causing the structure to collapse.

LET'S EXPLORE

1. Would a **lateral brace** increase the strength of the building and reduce the deforming flexibility? Repeat the experiment, placing a straw horizontally across the center of the frame.

2. How would a solid wall affect the strength and deforming flexibility of the structure? Solid walls connected to to a frame are called **shear-wall bracings**. To test their effect, repeat

the experiment while covering the original square frame with a piece of cardboard. Use tape to secure the cardboard to the frame. **Science Fair Hint:** As part of a project, display the shear-wall bracing model, as well as models representing a vertical and lateral braced frame. Include diagrams indicating the amount of flexibility of each structure.

LATERAL BRACE

SHOW TIME!

Buildings in earthquake areas that survive earthquakes must be able to bend without breaking. Test the flexibility of different strips of building material by securing each strip to a table with a "C" clamp. Add weights to the end of the strip by placing rocks in a pail attached to the end of the strip. Continue to add the rocks to the pail until the pail is full or the strip cracks. Display the various materials tested with a comparison of their flexibility.

CHECK IT OUT!

In choosing a metal support for a building, the elasticity and tensile strength of the metal must be considered. Define *tensile strength* and *elasticity*, and explain why they are especially important when selecting building supplies in earthquake areas.

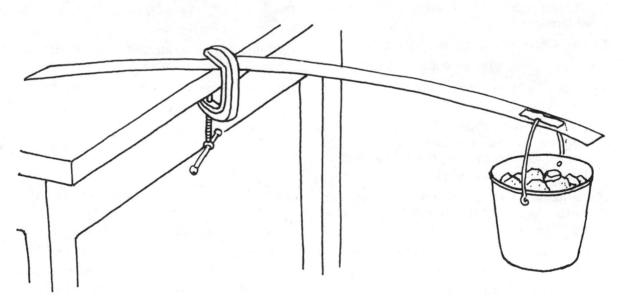

Glossary

Amplitude   Measurement of the height of an earthquake wave.

Bedrock   A rock formation under the ground.

Body waves   Seismic waves inside the earth.

Compressing   Decreasing the volume by pressing materials together.

Compression forces   Forces pushing toward each other from opposite directions.

Convection currents   Up-and-down cycle of movement caused by changes in the density of a material as a result of temperature differences.

Crust   Outer layer of the earth's surface.

Dampen   To deaden or stop vibrations.

Density   The number of molecules in a specific volume.

Dip-slip displacement   The up-and-down movement of rocks in the ocean that causes the water above the rocks to rise and fall with the moving sea bed.

Earthquake   Violent shaking of the earth caused by a sudden movement of rock beneath its surface.

Earthquake zones   Areas where earthquakes are most likely to occur.

Elastic limit   The point at which a stretched material loses elasticity and breaks.

Epicenter   The point on the earth's surface directly above the focus of an earthquake.

Fault   A break in the earth's crust.

Flexible   The ability of a material to bend or stretch without breaking.

Focus   The point at which earthquake vibrations begin.

Fractured   Cracked.

Friction   The resistance to motion; a force that pushes against a moving object, causing it to stop moving.

Hypocenter   The underground point of origin of an earthquake.

Hypothesis   An educated guess about the solution to a problem.

Inertia   Resistance to change in motion.

Intensity   A measurement of the effects an earthquake has on the land, the extent to which buildings are deformed, the number of people killed or injured, and any other changes.

Kinetic energy   Energy of motion having magnitude as well as direction.

Landfill   Land that has been built up by adding dirt, rocks, garbage, or other fillers.

Lateral   Sideways.

Lateral brace   A horizontal support between two vertical structures.

Lithosphere   The solid, outermost part of the earth; made up of the crust and the upper part of the mantle.

Lock fault   The point where two tectonic plates, because of friction, are temporarily locked together.

Love waves   Earthquake waves that move back and forth.

Lubricant   A slippery material that reduces friction.

Magma   Liquid rock.

Magnitude   Measurement of the amount of shaking energy released by an earthquake.

Mantle   The second layer of the earth's interior.

P-waves   Primary waves. The fastest and most energetic earthquake waves, which travel beneath the earth's surface at about 5 miles (8 km) per second.

Potential energy   Energy due to position.

Raleigh waves   Earthquake waves that move up and down.

Rebound   To snap or spring back into shape.

Reflect   To bounce back from a surface.

Refract   To change direction.

Richter scale   A number system used to measure the total shaking energy of an earthquake.

S-waves   Secondary waves. The slow earthquake waves that travel beneath the earth's surface at a speed of about 2 miles (3.2 km) per second.

Seismic sea waves   Giant sea waves caused by earthquakes. Often incorrectly called tidal waves. A common Japanese name for these waves is tsunamis.

Seismic waves   Earthquake vibrations.

Seismogram   A written record of the amount of shaking energy released by an earthquake.

Seismograph   An instrument that measures and records seismic waves produced by earthquakes.

Seismologist   A scientist who studies earthquakes.

Shear forces   Forces that push against an object from different directions, tearing the material apart.

Shear-wall bracing   Solid walls over a frame.

Sinkholes   Underground cavities dissolved in limestone rock.

Subduction zone   The area where sections of sinking lithosphere cause one tectonic plate to be pushed below another plate.

Tectonic plates   Huge, moving pieces of the lithosphere (outermost part of the earth).

Tension forces   Forces that push or pull a material apart.

Tidal waves   A common but incorrect name for giant sea waves. The correct name is seismic sea waves, or tsunamis.

Tsunamis   Japanese name for seismic sea waves.

Transverse waves   Seismic waves that cause rock particles to vibrate at right angles to the direction in which the wave is moving.

Transmission   To send out, as in the transmission (sending) of earthquake vibrations.

Vertical   Up-and-down direction.

Vibrate   To move back and forth.

Index

More Exciting and Fun Activity Books from Janice VanCleave...
Available from your local bookstore or simply use the order form below.

Mail to: Jennifer Bergman, John Wiley and Sons, Inc., 605 Third Avenue, New York, New York, 10158-0012

Title	ISBN	Price
__ ANIMALS	55052-3	$9.95
__ EARTHQUAKES	57107-5	$9.95
__ ELECTRICITY	31010-7	$9.95
__ GRAVITY	55050-7	$9.95
__ MACHINES	57108-3	$9.95
__ MAGNETS	57106-7	$9.95
__ MICROSCOPES	58956-X	$9.95
__ MOLECULES	55054-X	$9.95
__ VOLCANOES	30811-0	$9.95
__ ASTRONOMY	53573-7	$10.95
__ BIOLOGY	50381-9	$10.95
__ CHEMISTRY	62085-8	$10.95
__ DINOSAURS	30812-9	$10.95
__ EARTH SCIENCE	53010-7	$10.95
__ GEOGRAPHY	59842-9	$10.95
__ GEOMETRY	31141-3	$10.95
__ MATH	54265-2	$10.95
__ PHYSICS	52505-7	$10.95
__ 200 GOOEY, SLIPPERY. SLIMY, WEIRD, & FUN EXPERIMENTS		
	57921-1	$12.95
__ 201 AWESOME, MAGICAL. BIZARRE, & INCREDIBLE EXPERIMENTS		
	31011-5	$12.95

To Order
by Phone:

Call
1-800-225-5945

TOTAL: _____

[ ] Check/Money Order Enclosed
[ ] Charge my ___ Visa ___ Mastercard ___ AMEX ___ Discover
Card # _____ Exp. Date _____
(Wiley pays postage & handling on all prepaid orders)
NAME:_____
ADDRESS:_____
CITY:_____ STATE:_____ ZIP:_____
SIGNATURE:_____ (Offer Not Valid Unless Signed)

WILEY
Publishers Since 1807